COUNTRY OF GLASS

COUNTRY OF GLASS

Poems

Sarah Katz

Gallaudet University Press
Washington, DC

Gallaudet University Press
gupress.gallaudet.edu

Gallaudet University Press is located on the
traditional territories of Nacotchtank and Piscataway.

ISBN 978-1-954622-03-6 (paperback)
ISBN 978-1-954622-04-3 (ebook)

Library of Congress Cataloging-in-Publication Data
Names: Katz, Sarah (Sarah Bea), author.
Title: Country of glass : poems / Sarah Katz.
Description: Washington, DC: Gallaudet University Press, 2022. | Summary:
  "Country of Glass is the first collection of poetry by Sarah Katz"–
  Provided by publisher.
Identifiers: LCCN 2021048421 (print) | LCCN 2021048422 (ebook) | ISBN
  9781954622036 (paperback ; alk. paper) | ISBN 9781954622043 (ebook)
Subjects: LCGFT: Poetry.
Classification: LCC PS3611.A816 C68 2022 (print) | LCC PS3611.A816
  (ebook) | DDC 811/.6--dc23/eng/20211008
LC record available at https://lccn.loc.gov/2021048421
LC ebook record available at https://lccn.loc.gov/2021048422

∞ This paper meets the requirements of ANSI/NISO Z39.48–1992
(Permanence of Paper).

Cover description: Centered text (top to bottom, all in black): COUNTRY
OF GLASS (sans serif font); poems (script font); Sarah Katz (serif font).
The cover has a white background with three circles in varying sizes, with
varying shades of yellow. There are four shards of glass interspersed on the
cover.

Cover design by Eric C. Wilder.

CONTENT WARNING

Some poems in this collection explore sensitive material such as torture, sexual assault, terminal illness, murder, and war.

CONTENTS

PART ONE

PART TWO

PART THREE

We know no rules
of procedure,

we are voyagers, discoverers
of the not-known,

the unrecorded;
we have no map;

possibly we will reach haven,
heaven.

—"THE WALLS DO NOT FALL," *TRILOGY*, H.D.

PART ONE

It's so quiet in the world. One can hear the old river, which in its confusion sometimes forgets and flows backward.

—"THE DEAD MEN...," *THE WORLD DOESN'T END*, CHARLES SIMIC

The Hidden Country, I

Two woolly animals meet,
their bodies as luminous as stars.

But this stillness between them—
I don't understand.

Da Album

Bemel stole potatoes
    from a freight car
to survive
    Hantsavichy.

Great Grandma Sonia
    watched
as he dragged the sack
    past graves he dug
for other Jews,
    unaware her daughter Annia
would marry him.

That's not until New York,
    where the past
barely exists, but
    the pain lingers,
a ghost.

Until each night,
    my father listens
as Bemel and Annia hurl dishes
    at the walls before
he takes off
    to Jacksonville
in a yellow convertible.

Now, Granny Annia gestures
    to the girl
in the painting
    hugging twigs
in a Siberian sunset of fog.

"Leestin to me," she says,
    brushing her fire-red hair.

She applies coral lipstick
          onto her lips.
"Dis ees my only story."

I sit with the cracked-faced
          dolls on the sofa
as she talks.

"Your Great Grandma Sonia
          received Skippy
peanut butter
          from the Red Cross
and not knowing what eet vas, used eet
          to fill up cracks
in da apartment."

"Your Great Uncle Lou
          jumped out a window
with an umbrella
          thinking he could fly."

"When we left the camp for good,
          Mr. Nut, da cat,
cried after us, following the truck."

The kettle whistles on the stove
          as she begins
to play the accordion
          Lou brought
to another labor camp
          under his clothes.

"Da album, sveetie,"
          "Please get me da album."

Portrait of a Brother and Sister, 1940

She rides turtles across Siberian tundra.
Children shout in Polish from passing cattle cars.
Her brother strikes an angry driver with his gun,
who falls to the ground, mouth frothing like a dog's.
Run, he shouts to her with a coyote's eyes
narrow as dark seeds.

Her brother chases her to Kazakhstan wielding
a snake stick. Yellow eyes stalk them at night.
She is six. By twelve, she knows seven languages,
memorizes Aleksander Pushkin, sings operettas
in French and German. In New York, she shapes
new sounds with her tongue. Always,
her brother's stick follows closely.

How to Be a Child of War

Be five years old
on an ice road in Siberia.
To the left, mountains.
To the right, mountains.
It is -35 degrees.

Up above, your mother in the forest—
too thin to exist—
grinds a double-handed saw
across an oak
with another starved woman.

Watch from the road,
each tree, severing, crackling
under its newly uneven weight,
toppling from the mountain,
down into the Indigirka river.

Your mother who
has eaten nothing
but a slice of black bread.
Your mother, your mother.

The Beginning of Prayer

My father, tangled in the height of adolescence,
wept outside Old Saint Paul's Church as spring died,
reading Desiderata. The poem lay inscribed
in rock at the rear of the church, where
he counted his blessings. The sky,
he told me, was angry, angrier than most,
and I imagined billowy Michelangelos
swollen with inconsolable rain.

I was eight when he told the story late one night,
after dinner, after all candles had been blown out.
He stroked my back as I lay on his stomach,
burying myself into his large body, thinking
This is the moment I'm supposed to remember.
I watched his movements, listening to his pulse,
for what was coming, for what would soon be
the trickling of my own prayer.

One afternoon, my father awoke to a pounding
in his temples, to a plum-colored bruise
the size of a mango, spreading across his head
like a puddle. As his brain bled, my mother
stood outside the door at the hospital, waiting,
because this is what doctors recommend.
To wait. My sister looked out onto the parking lot,
the window streaked with black rain.

After he began to walk again, wobbling back
into the house with an almost-familiar smile,
I thought of what he had said all those years ago.
I thought of the swelling of the clouds, how
I thought it would never stop raining
after he'd come inside, carrying candlelight
that bloomed in every room,
and that I would never feel safe again
for as long as I prayed.

Portrait of My Deaf Body

He studies her like she's a flame that illuminates the universe

How do you do it? How do you live?

Bra snaps

I dress undress piss sometimes I eat

But you are something else

She pulls him into his bed

This is how my mother saved me
And my eyes are from my father
I have held death with this hand

Lifts her right hand

I have many sisters
They all look like me

He bites her lip

No, it can't be

Licks the curves of her stomach like an icy spoon

The End of the Ordinary Body, I

After the accident,
I was redrawn in light,

my body a suit.

Blossom of blood
at my feet.

Rupture revealed bone,

salt-crusted skin.
Smoldered through me

like memory.

Tinsel's gleam
and rubber peeling away.

I couldn't speak.

The sag of being.
The car's fragmenting: a thief.

Memory

after Charles Simic

Great was the apartment.
The goat that roamed its rooms,
dreamed in a bed of hay.
The voices steeped in borscht,
the voices that don't return.
Spilled pillars of spice.

I am the first child here.
Seventy years have passed.
The forests' arms still break my eyes.
I still run with crooked fingers.
I still want answers.
A book of Pushkin
to wear like a hat.

Poland, scatter your music.
I have no fingers. You'll
have to whisper it into my ears.
My ears are dead.
You'll have to carve it into me
one number at a time.

Post-Craniotomy

You appear dehorned
with two holes on your head—

an unsuspected devil
newly redeemed. Your eyes

stay closed. Seated on the bed,
I watch your broad face shrink

into a new country.
Your forehead perspires.

Under the plate of your chest,
your red heart sinks and rises,

body closed, motionless.
The unknown world there

bothers me, so I superimpose
the idea of your eyeballs

onto the fact of your face.
For a moment, you stare back,

I think, black ponds trickling
into my own. But it is me

staring from the internal mirror,
wandering without a map.

Photograph of the Philippine General Hospital, 1905

Black water rolls through the hospital's arches
into Taft Avenue as terracotta roof tiles
slide into the new river
while four men search for a way out of it

One pushes his body with all limbs
so much river water dripping
off his chin
one could confuse his expression for crying

Two others in the bow and stern of a rowboat
point their salakót hats forward
Muscled arms folding inward and outward
they jab and pull long oars
propelling the boat onward

A fourth leads the rest, naked
his expression mute and river-gray
his legs foreshortened at the knee
immobile as a photograph

There will be a rescue I'm sure of it
but before the men are set free again
the tributary strays downhill
through rice paddy terraces
people and flat stones

The Hidden Country, II

His skin one hundred years old,
and with the rheumy flare
of the measuring eye,
Grandpa says: *How will it end?*
These are his final words.

Meanwhile, trout so iridescent
they seem our brothers,
hold their gaze toward the light
of what we do not see,
riverwater scrawling
a country on their backs.

PART TWO

*"I can't remember the tale,
but hear his voice still, a well
of dark water, a prayer."*

—"THE GIFT," *ROSE*, LI-YOUNG LEE

Dream of Arrival

Over there, the crabapple tree juts from an oasis—her pink fruit accessible only to the water- and air-borne—and under reflections of Scottish pine, her half-sunk roots hemorrhage and roil. Here, two sneakered feet watch, bone-hard rocks slipping into chiseled oblivion. You've returned from somewhere far away, haven't you, Tree? It's a world I am learning.

Amulet

As our father's brain bleeds, we hunt for gifts in the hospital shop. This one, I say, holding up a pin for my brother and sister to see: IT'S A BOY. We snort and our chests tighten. I buy the pin and a large package of macadamia nut cookies. When it's my turn to visit our father, I brush the cookie crumbs off my shirt and push through the double doors, gripping a circle in my pocket.

Portrait of Childhood, I

Velvet eggs line my mother's bathroom shelves. *Leave my things alone*, she'd said after I had broken her earring dishes or stolen a piece of her jewelry. I'd nodded remorsefully. Now, the crimson-colored egg, lined yellow and gold in places, opens like a hatchback—or a mouth—the top gently yielding backward. *Fwip*. I look inside. Six baby teeth, all mine.

Portrait of Childhood, II

You love that bug juice our father says as we guzzle ice-water mixed with Crystal Light at the picnic table. *Bug juice*, we all consider vaguely, as though our drink is suffused with bug-corpses crushed finely, then crossed with the flavor of cherry. Macabre? Somehow, we don't think so, even if we fake-gag. *Bug juice.* Yes, the three of us chirrup, staring slack-jawed at the blood-red drink, the thought soon disappearing as we down the last few swigs. The mix pools in our stomachs redly, our seven- and nine-year-old lips gluing and ungluing with pink spit and sugar, the too-bright sun painting thin rainbows on our vision.

Haven

Jagged pine trees stark against the white sky. A girl places a note under a stone swarming with potato bugs, and holding her palms against the slate, says, *You'll take care of it?* The growing grass under her floral dress silent, with only a squirrel stopping by to look at her with a nut in his hands, shocked.

Escape

My feet carry me toward the edge of the woods, but no trees or leaves or shrubs scratch through me, just thoughts I see, until, peripherally, I catch a plane's descent, then a great, thundering light—which shakes and undoes my balance. Then—snap—a twig—and, inside, a snap of another kind, the crumpling bodies ahead inscrutable. Well before I leave the woods, there is the loss of everyone I know.

Vow

—*Will you still love me when I am different?* my father breathes between seizures, a moon egg face, his skull full of staples and blood. I pick at my sneakers on the bleached floor of the intensive care unit and smile until he opens his eyes, slips on his shoes, and totters home, where our family thereafter forgets how to speak to each other. Silence grows shrill and tangled, throttling every wall of the house and interstice between. I escape through the kitchen one night, the screen door pattering *pit pat pat* behind me, to a willow weeping in the wavering spark of the moon. I hum and brush glossy strands of willow hair straight with my fingers. Cry *yes.*

The End of the Ordinary Body, II

Pain-sweat escapes my father's great forehead, clear as a returning memory of malady, and so vision blurs in defense of the ordinary body. Pain's unpardonable. Pain's proportional. Empathy, in low supply. And diffidence, the lesser of two evils. *You're not ill,* The Doctor said. *You're not ill,* The Daughter said. *I love you,* we say, our eyes half-shut. *But don't look at me. I don't want to be found or helped or loved.* A teenager confronts the reflection of the hunger artist. In the supermarket, she distributes pamphlets on pain.

Haze

The child doesn't take her mother's emotional distance personally. *The woman is going through a lot right now*, she says to herself in the silence of her bedroom, surrounded by stuffed animals and dolls as if at a support group meeting. The dolls stare, their attentions so focused upon her, that she can't be sure whether or not they are real.

Dream of Exile

We—a group of fugitives and I—attempt to bury ourselves to escape someone's wrath. Everyone tries to bury me first, for some reason. I assist halfheartedly, because I would really like to spruce up before resigning myself to six feet under. I would prefer more lipstick and more nail polish, and I am choosy about which. At some point I realize that everyone is trying to steal my jewelry. That's when I decide I don't want to be buried after all.

Lessons in Isolation

In the prison, bodies come to understand the walls. Their hands move little, clutched in front of faces until there is the wall and the barred window of the cell. From behind there, you can sense other hands slithering past like amoebas, unseen and immune to expression, but they are there, hidden, all five fingers faintly moving. Silence, at least, at last, will never leave. Yes, there is the door, but outside it, the soundless jangling of people.

Unidentified Man

The red-bearded man does not stand with his sign at this same intersection every day. Sometimes he stands at a different intersection where the scenery is less pleasant, being grayer, and with too many cars driving swiftly past. In any case, most everyone who passes through these two intersections while on the way to work sees the man at least once a week. No one knows his name, but everyone will say that he has seen him.

Superstition

The horse is just galloping along through the woods when he comes across another horse's leg splayed out on a bed of leaves and separated from the horse it belonged to. Aghast at the plainness of the coarse-haired hock— its incontrovertible corporeality—the horse softly neighs to himself: *legs absolutely must be attached to the torso*. The horse returns to his village to discuss the matter with his friends, who all vigorously agree that this finding by the first horse is horrid, absolutely horrid. The horse leg forthwith becomes a symbol of disharmony, which now appears in the dreams of all god-fearing horses.

Family Meal

Boris, the goat, makes a typical *maaa-ing* noise, grunting when children approach to pet his coarse brown-and-black hair. The look in his eye is one of indifference at first glance: a black ball that coolly registers images. If you get close enough, however, you'll notice Boris's downturned mouth. Sometimes, this is accompanied by one tear in the corner of Boris's left eye. If you listen at the shed door, you can hear his shuddering sobs.

The Sun's Song

The sun is reaching for my eyes, the unseasonable heat droning on and on about itself. Aglow on the tops of everything, of cars passing. People stumbling through the parking lot through it, looking for someone or a place waiting for them. The wind shivers in the trees. The sun wishes to be known the way I want to be hidden.

Leaving the Village

So stupid, Mama and Tata can't decide what to take, the hats or the silver, as bomby turn other houses into flames. Outside, Danusha waits with her matka in a long yellow sundress. Danusha, Danusha, I squawk from the eleventh apartment window, but she doesn't budge, acts like she can't hear me, doesn't know me from Tata. Her body dim, something I can't touch, like fire or shadow. We're going, I shout to the statue of Danusha. This time she turns around and looks up at me with eyes blacker than blood-soaked dirt. What can I say? When Mama and Tata have stopped arguing, Danusha and her mother have disappeared. Then we are running, Mama's hand over my eyes. Something like samoloty above us open fire, tick tick tick tick tick, and I am pushed upon the raining ground. When I open my eyes again, we are in a forest with sticks in our mouths. The trees shudder like they are coming alive.

Scene of Death

Ice-tensed, the trees stab branches to sky with something of deadness, the leaves quiet, and not one man awake. There is no pulling down this canvas, the figures deeply drawn. It pricks the eyes, scratching and breaking. There is a crack of yolk. It drips from the lip of some bowl.

The Forest's Song

The trees mute the sky with crosshatching branches, or they mute each other, producing a spreading silence. Get me out, a voice says: a man, pinioned by stillness. Alas, no hands reach from this wilderness. He huffs air-vapors, to prove his standing to the woods. *I am here. My shadow cool upon the leaves.*

Photograph of Swimmers in Prague, 1912

Three men gaze down at a woman lying on river grass. The woman smiles in a white dress, the ground flat under the curve of her bottom. One man, bending his elbows, straps on his suspenders. Another contorts his body into an L to roll up his trousers. Two ignored children in dresses look on, their heads mysteriously shaved.

Intent

Come right back, he recalls his mother saying as he exited the apartment. Nearly a hundred Pollacks milled around the American Red Cross tent, squinting through the sun and awaiting their bread. The boy acquired his loaf, which was sheathed in crinkling plastic. It was so white it could have been the ass of a swan.

Here We Are

The bread held up, an offering to the gods. Most of the men pray, the women kneeling, their hands clasped together. The children talk to themselves through the mess of eyelashes, immersed in a soft, honeyed light. *Here we are*, they whisper, as they turn over black bread that chafes their little hands.

PART THREE

*"from this point on, the silence through which you move
is my voice pursuing you."*

—"QUIET EVENING," *MEADOWLANDS*, LOUISE GLÜCK

Country of Glass

I dreamt I was alone with the baby grand,
your porcelain vases facing the window
as if they didn't want to see me. My life, yours,
with the boneless chicken dinners from a box,
the tatty pink toothbrushes by the kitchen sink,
the red hair dye on the bedroom bookshelf.
When I woke, I saw nothing changed:
the usual head of blonde hair in my bed,
the white voile curtains behind him,
the lump of his body encased in blankets.
Yet something had shifted.
I stripped down, laid down in the cold bathtub,
tried to decide what to care about.
Maybe it was the dream before this dream
that made everything seem a country of glass:
my own black molars sparking into small pieces.

Torture

In the era of
                torture,

            we

    strip   everything

                        authorize

                                cold water
                                        rape
                sodomizing
    biting

                                        smiling.

        the bloodied body

a riot

at

our door

the chest

against

isolation

The   body

's defense

system

the smooth operation of
a   state

.

o

                                                    Loosen
                        the

                chain
        the wing

                                        shackled

reject

its soldiers

                                        the

        the world
's
                                sins.

—SEYMOUR M. HERSH, "TORTURE AT ABU GHRAIB," THE NEW YORKER

Although We Cannot Go Back

"The photographs tell it all. In one, Private England, a cigarette dangling from her mouth, is giving a jaunty thumbs-up sign and pointing at the genitals of a young Iraqi, who is naked except for a sandbag over his head, as he masturbates."

—SEYMOUR M. HERSH, "TORTURE AT ABU GHRAIB," *THE NEW YORKER*

Let us two leave it all behind bury
the hatchet the photographs
your dreams of choking
on an American's cock

or the shit spreading on your tongue
into your thinning eyes
as you forget your family your body
the only remainder

but of what

Let us two open your palm of blood
that we cannot wash away but
let us imagine your souvenir
of pain winging

doves of peace

Let us pretend for a moment
this never happened

That even though we could
we would not leave marks
that do not come from love

Would you have placed
your mouth on mine called me
by my name.

And what would my name from your mouth say.

Would it say I made this for you.

Would it say.

They Fall Apart

You piece the shapes of my mouth together
tracing messages, my constellations
bounding deer. You don't hear me yell
until I hold your palm to my throat.
Sound is funny. We laugh at the words.
They get in the way, odd winged things.

Words dart around us for nothing.
We snicker at those lassoing them together
because all for what? Tangled words
march away into air, constellations
wilder than lightning. We watch others yell,
incensed, thrusting thunder from their throats

and laugh, leaping into the hill's throat
behind the school, gathering lilacs, pretty things
we want to remember. School bells yell
to return. Children gather together
like wolves. In dirt, we sketch constellations.
Their mouths must hurt from so many words.

You think maybe they don't. *Give me their words!*
your mouth says. A cracking in my throat.
I don't want to fight with constellations
too hard to see. *There are greater things*
I say, *things that fit well together,*
that don't fall apart. But still you yell,

Give me the words! I'm tired of your yell.
I point to their lips. *You read the words.*
You look with your O mouth, your O throat,
squinting and the sounds fly away together,
blurring by, dying constellations
we cannot see. They look like nothings.

Our eyes hurt at the sight of nothings
their mouths shape. We map lips and yells
flashing by, ineffable constellations,
stitching together their half-words,
craters in the dark. We feel together
for thunder, sewing symbols to their throats

for nothing. They get in the way, their throats
tangling the air with wayward words,
the signs never right, never falling together.

The End of Being Delicate

"About 47 to 65 million years ago, the Seychelles broke off from the supercontinent
Gondwana—one of two land masses comprising the supercontinent Pangaea—
splitting the [Gardiner's] frogs off from other species. So hearing through the mouth
may actually be a holdover from ancient life-forms, the authors say."

—NATIONAL GEOGRAPHIC

On my pinky fingernail, the Gardiner's frog swallows
an unapologetic hurricane of breath.

You are so tiny, I whisper to it,
sound thumping its rubbery, frogly head,

the "i" in "tiny" not tiny as a breadcrumb,
but as an eye in a keyhole that stares

as if it knows embarrassing things about you.
I think I am being gentle. I think

I have gentle thoughts about gentle things,
but my awkward voice fumbles over skin

its mouth's ridges jerking back
a layer over a hole of throat.

Open and Open

Dear brother,
I want the truth in the amber

bottle, empty, beside you. The vomit
that sealed your lips.

The abundance of you and your addiction,
and the decay. I want you open

to a wholeness between us.
Not this fissure. Not this blank country

shorn of what is true. I want
the weight of your truth

to arrive the way that bright summer
afternoon and its black SUV

pinned me to asphalt,
opening fresh holes in my body.

Brother, the body's only promise
is that it will open—

so much depends on this openness.
The wholeness of what is broken.

Widowed

for Joan, my grandmother

You cackled at the young man's jokes
nearly 35 years his senior.
Your husband died and you could do that.

A blankness in the mouth, a froth
of spittle and inflamed ears.
It isn't that you didn't love him

but the weight of him had lifted
and you were you.
Shadows still lingered expectant;

you could even see them better now.
Everything on the vanity, curved.
The hand mirror had split, you knew

by the blood on your fingers.
But what did it matter now?
A faceless hurt surrounds the body

the knife always digging,
and now the bedroom music
worming through your head.

The Living Room

Here is the rich room I sit in.
The leather chair that rocks under my weight.
The light that glistens from the doll
on the mantle, hitting the eyes as circles.

Such objects breathe,
the brown lamp twirling its dress,
the television another presence
that lived before me.

Now, the chair warms my bottom,
and my bottom warms the chair.
It heaves its metal and fibers onto me,
my skin of joint and bone digging into it.

Is this the room's own waiting?
Or is its silence a hole I crawl through?
The sky outside drains itself of color.
The trees, stripping down to their silhouettes.

You can touch me sky.
I will only believe the wind in my hair.

Light and Dark Country

for Joan

Tree shadows meet with light on the wall of the house
battling over shifting divisions of shaded country
the adjacent green-mass always whole and trembling.

They drop their leaves that I sweep off the picnic table
with the acorns also fallen. You're the perfect colors
in the leaves beneath me, aren't you?—the chlorophyll bleeding

toward the creased edges, the curl like a cupped hand, crumbling
and dry as my throat was when I had descended the hill that day,
leaving a stranger's house, clothes loose, feet crunching the earth to bits.

Why does anyone do anything? The trees just blow in the wind.

A Room We Have Never Stood In

Under a net of urban sky,
wheels whelp on asphalt,

the wheelchair hoisting up
the weakened arms and legs

of a boy. He's my father,
aged ten, the sickness just arrived.

Rheumatoid arthritis, he explained
once, the words evading his tongue.

His boy face is thick-browed,
a suppler mimic of older bodies.

Annia, his mother, rolls him
through the city over shocks

of ache, until enough rest
suffices and he escapes

with his boyhood. Years later,
he's forty-nine, on the gurney,

and I, his daughter, watching him
roll away into a room

we have never stood in before.
The child that lingered in him

resurfaces through the pores
of his wide forehead

where his skin purples
by the constant mole

that neighbors his left eye.
Subdural hematoma.

My father's shrinking body,
too perceptible in fluorescent

light as it seizes, newly epileptic,
shakes my own.

The End of Childhood

Once, you were my father,
head bent over yellow legal pads,
an oblong office around you,
working out your life.

Now you are my father, sweat
gathering on your wide forehead.
At the window, I watch you wrench weeds
from unyielding, dark mud.

Ruin

You've noticed how
we lack bodies
in the ruined place.

We no longer harvest
one another's eyes,
the windows to ruin.

Back before I loved you,
I love you arrived
before it meant itself,

a package of unripe
fruit. We swooned
over each other's

chicken-skin, odd light
swilling in our skulls.
Night's ineffable feathers

prickled us. Then,
our footfalls fading,
lolling over landscapes

of bone flooded by blood
rivers, you whispered
something unmemorable

which set both our insides
aflame. When we arrived,
our limbs had vanished,

and the sky had riven
our faces open, hot world
yolking through.

Beyond Reykjavik

"The mastery of nature (so the imperialists teach) is the purpose of all technology."
—WALTER BENJAMIN

No future lives in our tundra.
No snatches of green.
Mount Hekla crowns miles
of ashen dirt
but occasionally,
arctic willows spume
from the earth's scorch
bright natives
of our Monochrome.

How we are sick
of the natives.
How pitifully superior
we feel
to the one-inched trees.
How unbearably lost
in the remaining dark,
existing as exiles.

An igneous rock
with its many eyes
in hand. It conjures up
cigarettes in our mouths
their red inhale.

But now we blink
toward endings.
We'd die with this place
at the wrong place wrong time
our wishes very crumbly
Pompeii firmly
grasping our feet
with its many hands.

ACKNOWLEDGMENTS

Thanks to the editors of the following journals for publishing the poems that appear in this book, including earlier versions:

District Lit (online and print): "The Beginning of Prayer." Winner of the 2015 District Lit Prize.

So to Speak (online): "Portrait of My Deaf Body," "Although We Cannot Go Back," "They Fall Apart."

Rogue Agent (online): "The End of the Ordinary Body, I."

MiPOesias (print/online): "Memory."

The Shallow Ends (online): "Post-Craniotomy."

Bear Review (print/online): "Photograph of the Philippine General Hospital, 1905."

From the Depths (print/online): "Vow."

Rhino (print): "Leaving the Village."

Right Hand Pointing (online): "Dream of Exile."

Redivider Journal (print/online): "Lessons in Isolation."

Public Pool (online): "Unidentified Man," "Superstition," "Photograph of Swimmers in Prague, 1912."

Temenos (print): "The End of Being Delicate."

Wordgathering (online): "Open and Open."

I'm grateful for the support of my family, friends, and teachers. Thank you to those who read and reread my poems before their completion: Kyle Dargan, Daniel Ginsberg, David Keplinger, Greg Luce, Holly Mason, Susan Mockler, Alison Palmer, and Adam Pollack. Thanks to Robert Pinsky for seeing promise in an earlier version of my manuscript. Cheers to the good people at Gallaudet University Press. And thank you, Jonathan, my light.

ABOUT THE AUTHOR

Sarah Katz's poems have appeared in *District Lit*, the *So to Speak* blog, *Rogue Agent*, *MiPOesias*, *The Shallow Ends*, and *Bear Review*, among others. She has contributed essays and articles to a variety of publications, including *The Atlantic*, *The Guardian*, *The New York Times*, *The Washington Post*, *The Rumpus*, *Slate*, and others. She lives in Fairfax, Virginia, with her husband.